The Deconstruction and Reconstruction of
YOU

The Deconstruction and Reconstruction of

YOU

by Dr. Samone M. Smith Brown

ACHKNOWLEDGEMENTS

Author: Dr. Samone M. Smith-Brown

The Deconstruction and Reconstruction of
YOU

Editor: Belinda James - info@BelindaTrotterJames.com

Book Cover Design - Sean Strong- seanstrong.com

DEDICATION

To my husband, Bruce Brown... You have been my lover, my friend, my rock, my cheerleader, the man who calms my storms. This book is dedicated to the blessing that was bestowed upon me in 2002 when we first met. Thank you for never giving up on me, for telling me the truth when others would only tell me what they thought I wanted to hear. GOD makes no mistakes and with you, this is made evident.

To my smart, loving, talented daughter and #1 fan, Sydney A. Brown. You, my precocious angel, are one of the reasons I try so hard to make my dreams a reality. I want you to see that life may not always be easy, but it is worth making it what you want it to be. You make me smile when I am unhappy, and your hugs and kisses are the medicine my soul needs to heal when it is broken. I love you.

To Samuel Christopher Moses Smith... Thank you for being my brother, confidant and best friend. You are an inspiration to my life.

To my parents, Samuel and Charlene Smith. I thank you both for your guidance, love, support and for teaching me to follow my passions and path that has led me to where I am today. Without the lessons I've learned and my experiences, I would not have the vision to make it this far.

To my grandparents and my wonderful in-laws, I still hear and feel your guidance, love, and presence every day. To be gone from the earth is to be present with the Lord. Enjoy paradise.

MY GIFT TO YOU

This book is for all of us who have been hurt, cheated, told we weren't and would never be good enough. To all of you who yearn for a better life but feel that the path to happiness may be nonexistent or simply that we are not worth the journey. To those who have given of yourselves to so many, only to be left depleted by those we've given to who are now full. Take this book and all that it delivers and feed it to your spirit and adopt it as your own for you have helped me have the courage to write this book for you. This is your MANIFESTO!

TABLE OF CONTENT

INTRODUCTION

This is a book designed especially for YOU. This book will take you on a journey to learn about and subsequently fall in love with the wonderful individual living inside of you; the 'you' that you felt was impossible to achieve. This book will attempt to be your guide to the deconstruction of the old you and the exciting reconstruction of that hidden treasure deep inside.

This new journey is going to be fantastic! It will take you through some of your greatest efforts but will also provide some of the greatest personal fulfillment you've ever experienced to date. You will be transforming right before your very eyes. As such, this journey will not only make you uncomfortable at times but may also have the tendency to make those in your circle uncomfortable as well. In fact, it may surprise you to find out who in your life is genuinely happy for your reconstruction and those who you thought were your most staunch supporters with their "positive praises" whether from long ago or in your recent past, fall by the wayside. Basically, it's those people in your life who told you what you wanted to hear, but, never thought you would start, let alone accomplish your goals and transform. This time around you are going to reach your goals for yourself and be a force to be reckoned with. There will be some folk that may fall away, but just remember that for a plant to grow the weeds must be plucked first.

Some of those people will be those who have seen you start and stop projects or quests for enlightenment in the past and are looking upon you with the feelings of "here we go again... another project". Well, let them look, for you will prove them wrong this time. Remember your past actions do not and will not determine your future direction if and only if you put the work in needed for change to occur.

Remember, the word "work" is an action word, a verb. It requires action and when there is action, there will be results. Also, understand that your actions will cause reactions. Reactions from not only your spirit but also from those around you. Strangers will see you for the first time as your reconstructed self while those who were there before the reconstruction will have to adjust and accept the new, unstoppable, capable, positive, strong, amazing you that has emerged from who you once were. Some may not be able to take you at 100 proof, but it is also not for you to feel you must water yourself down for their comfort or approval. Where did that get you in the past?

The reality is that the more work you do, something is going to happen. A change will occur if you stay consistent. I'm sure you've been told that standing still in the silence of your goals also brings about change. It's true in some cases. It's all about the energy you give out into the universe.

However, in this case, the only thing that will happen without working and movement is that you will remain unchanged. When you stop moving, you will see your life, opportunities, happiness, growth, and goals pass you by. It's a terrifying thought to have a life left unlived, and undiscovered. It will turn out to be not a life at all, but a mere existence. What a sad thought. But let's get back to the reason for this book. This book is will be your reinforcement! Your hand-held personal weapon against staying stagnant. Use it as support when you encounter those whom you thought would remain by your side for the long haul but haven't. This book is filled with affirmations, exercises and words that are meant to feed your soul, uplift your spirit, and aid in the rediscovery of the buried person inside of you. Most importantly, this book was written to aid in your process of deconstruction and reconstruction.

Again, let's say this together: EVERYONE WILL NOT BE A FAN! Some may even turn against you. They may shake your confidence and cause you to want to reconsider all your actions. They may get into your mind so deeply with lies and guilt that you may begin to question and dislike yourself. They may even make you feel as if you are selfish to want to forge ahead with your rediscovery and reconstruction. But just remember these two things: 1. Even haters and naysayers have a job to do so we can't fault them for doing their job and 2. When they loathe you, that's when you love you with all your might.

You are an amazing movement of power backed by the powerful resilience of the mythical Phoenix! With every step, you take on each tile or paved street you tread, OWN IT! If anyone asks you "who do you think you are?", simply answer with the thunder of 1000 lightning strikes, "I Am the master of all that I touch! I Am the ruler of my destiny."

3

Now, take my hand as we embark on this journey of new self-discovery for I will not leave you until you are ready to take your first steps towards your solo flight among the Eagles! Your time of being a grounded pigeon or landfowl is over! Trust me, you will get there because YOU are worth it! Are you ready my friend?

Don't be afraid of change. Change is the metamorphosis of new beginnings to emerge.

Chapter 1
My Destruction

"In dealing with backstabbers, there was one thing I learned... They're only powerful when you got your back turned."

~ Eminem

As I sit here, in the dank basement of a place dubbed teacher jail, facing countless accusations and charges stemming from freedom of speech, I began to wonder why? Why would someone hate my very existence so much that she, yes, she, without any thought about the present or future of not only the students I took great care in molding or the life of my young daughter or the health of my fragile mother who has taken care of my incapacitated brother for over a year stab me in the back?

My brother, once strong and virile has been unable to move or speak after having a cardiac arrest at the young age of 39. This backstabbing woman didn't have any regard for the career that I worked so hard to build. In one moment, this woman decided that her hatred of me, which runs so deep, meant more to her than the countless lives being interrupted. The fire of her burning rage just had to be quenched. This is very sad for as they say people who have deep issues within themselves many times will fight their battles by attacking others. So, through her actions, I was knocked temporarily off my steady perch. However, during the hurt, I had to find peace and forgiveness. I had to search deep within myself and see past what she did. I had to find the lesson and the positive energy in it all. It was hard. I did not retaliate, nor did I feel it inside to do so.

I know this struggle sounds very familiar to many of you who are reading this because you too have been attacked and blindsided. You too have trusted people and thought they were your friends only to find out that they wished and plotting your demise.

I had, at the time of writing this, been a teacher for almost 20 years, never once getting into trouble, never once being transferred, but now, because I dared to be me, I was penalized. I say all of this to say, yes this is a book about being authentically, unapologetically, fiercely you, but many times that has a price. Sometimes, as in my case, a very high price. However, the question is, do you stop being you to make others happy and comfortable about the skin they are in or do you go through the fires, the cuts, and scrapes to be shaped into the diamond you truly are?

Ask yourself how many times were you misrepresented and instead of fighting back and being brave enough to live your truth you sat silently and later agreed to and supported what they said about you? How long did you live in that self-imposed prison? How many times did you adopt the fears, failures and misrepresentations placed upon you by what others said? How often did you let it chip away at your self-esteem, your self-worth, and visions of your future? How often did it rob you of the happiness that you could share with yourself and others? Think about how often it caused you to miss the opportunity to live in the amazing true authentic glory of being simply you?

I had to oftentimes ask myself those questions and realized that many times in the past I was too afraid to do anything about it. It was easier to live in that prison than to shout out my truths and take charge of my life. It's always easier not to ruffle any feathers on the outside but not so true about ruffling your feathers on the inside. I learned this from a very early age.

It began with the first time I was touched without being asked, the first time, at the tender age of 5 when I was molested. In each chapter, I will lay bare my soul. I will be transparent throughout

the book for you to see different times in my life when I faced destruction. Those times in my life where it was the darkest and at a time in my life where I wanted to take my own life.

Many times, especially when your world looks and feels the darkest, our instincts tell us to run, hide, or sulk. We feed into the negative thoughts of those who try to describe our character. We begin to adopt the vision, the movie script, the version of ourselves that others are so perfectly painting, for the hurt and the heartbreak zaps our strength and with that, the ability to fight. We neglect the fight because we see ourselves as, in some way, the cause of the slings and arrows being thrown. However, in all honesty, we are better than that. It's easy to focus on the negative because we may view the positive as just chance or good luck. We neglect to see it as blessings and acknowledgment for whom we are building ourselves to be.

As the tears were being held back as I began to write this book, I was at a very low point. When my enemy was revealed to me, little did I know that I was winning. She was reveling in her destruction while the helicopters crashed above me and the carnage below me burned. I had to try to find the good in it all. For if I gave her back all that she was giving me then the cycle would have continued. If I needed to grow and wanted to grow, I had to realize that I had to let her, and every situation related to my turmoil fall away. It would have been easy to go and give an eye for an eye, but that would have left both of us blind. In that instance I realized that for me to get where I needed to go I needed clear vision. I needed both of my eyes.

"God changes caterpillars into butterflies, sand into pearls and coal into diamonds using time and pressure. He is working on you too."

A diamond is a precious and sometimes unattainable possession. We see diamonds as a sign of brilliance and elevation. However, what we fail to realize is at first that diamond was just an ugly, black, worthless lump of coal. It took the fire, the chipping away at its surface and the keen eye of a miner to see the beauty that is encapsulated. We must look at ourselves as diamonds. We must see that many times the hardships, trials, tribulations, and setbacks are all delivered to us to chip away at our surfaces. They are meant to transform us into the diamonds that lie within us. If you just let those trials and tribulations on the outside transform you on the inside, there will come a day that those experiences will illuminate your path. However, they will do so from the inside out (not outside-in). We must envision ourselves as diamonds. Diamonds in the rough. Lumps of coal worthy of being mined.

Oh but, how hard is it to do that especially when we live in a world that lives for worldly things. A world which has the keys to supply your peace whether it be with love, compassion, relationships, employment, status, and success. Or the converse: hatred, coldness, loneliness, low self-worth, emptiness, fear and imposed failure just for being you. For your sake and mine, I am going to pour my heart into this book. The chapters are short and meaty to get right to the point. However, I am a firm believer that if you have something of substance to say you don't have to draw it out. We live in a time where things are moving fast, and our attention spans are shorter anyway so getting to the point isn't such a bad thing.

Maybe the reason I feel the need to pour my heart into this book is because it will become my cathartic breakthrough. It will help with the unburdening of the hurt that I am going through now as I write this book and have gone through before. I haven't felt like life would be better off without me for some time. When I was at that point it was one of the lowest and darkest of my life. I found myself laying in a bed in the dark with just the light of the TV to illuminate my pills in one hand and the water in the other. As the TV flickered, so would my life have done the same if I would have swallowed those pills. The plan seemed like the only option and it was befitting a life of darkness, despair, molestation, physical abuse, loneliness, worthlessness, and confusion. I didn't feel lovable although I tried to love everyone else. No one would have missed me and it wouldn't have made a difference if I stayed or left this earth. There was no room for discussion for it was time. Yes, I planned to take my life.

As I lifted the bottle to my lips something said to wait. Before you end your life think about the impact ending your life would have on those around you. I began to see my brother and my mother crying over my casket, the children that I would never have, the sunshine I would never feel again, and honestly not knowing if I would even make it into heaven because from what I've learned taking your own life is a sin. For one moment even with thinking and visualizing those things I still contemplated just going ahead and doing it. But thank GOD I didn't.

At the time of putting these words down on paper, I felt like the world was swallowing me up. Like if there was an open mouth of a volcano I would have contemplated throwing myself into it to appease the gods. I know many of you have felt like this at some point in your lives. As you try to hold onto hope, you realize that the things you are going through are being done to you because you wanted to, tried to, and dared to be authentically you. There have been times where we have all been in the darkness of our own fear; cold, shaking and doubting who we are and what we want, but trust me you will rise! I realized that I had to rise because I could not allow or even fathom knowing that there are others out there who are in this cold desolate place and unsure how to elevate from the abyss. I don't want anyone reading this to be trapped in this dismal state. That person within you, that dream that is lying dormant within has every right to blossom just as you have every right to follow your own path.

Being authentically you should come with having no apologies. It's like those quotes that reference not being afraid to shine because the sun doesn't care who it blinds or in looking at yourself as a flower because a flower doesn't worry about the flower next to it, for it does what is in its nature to do....Bloom!

These quotes are telling us to be ourselves. To live our lives authentically. To be unapologetic about being our true self. All of this sounds so wonderful on paper and in theory. However, doing so out loud on your own terms, in the open when there are judging eyes is not only a different story, but it's also very hard.

It's magnified exponentially when those around you whether in your circle or those looking at you on the fringes feel threatened, angry or basically just have their own hate for you that becomes all-consuming. This makes it even more difficult to find the courage to be yourself.

I believe you are not destined to live with the foul of the ground while your wings clearly are of the caliber, strength, length, and beauty of a majestic eagle. If I allow you to live beneath your means and your greatness, to believe what is being told to you to dim your shine, to inhibit your metamorphosis, then you have lost, and I have failed you. If traveling the road of despair is one that I must yet tread down again, so be it. What doesn't kill you only makes you stronger and whatever makes you stronger promotes growth, remember that. Like I always say, everything may not be great, but in everything, something great can be found. I cannot be a hypocrite. If I talk the talk, I too must walk the walk. Even as I sit here reminiscing about times where I could neither talk nor walk I feel a burning inside. I believe it's a new awakening that comes from my excitement in knowing that you are about to take a long-awaited journey and although it may not always be easy, the result is going to be fabulous! You are well worth it! Please remember that. Repeat this to yourself as you do the exercises in this book. As you reminisce and as you deconstruct what others have built-in your life that serves you no good, continually say I AM worth it.

Whatever people think about you is not your business. This saying is true but once those thoughts turn into actions to dim your shine, it then becomes something tangible. It becomes a weapon used to diminish your light, to knock you off your horse, to show the crimps in your armor. When those arrows pierce your skin, it is up to you to figure out whether you fall to the ground and bleed to death or if you bandage yourself up, take care of the wounds and get back to the battle that is this thing called life. True, some scars are deeper than others and may take more time from which to heal and recover, but the result of getting up and not laying there bleeding out is recovery. You will eventually recover, but if you lay there and bleed out, you will die because your life force depletes, and you no longer have a chance.

So, without further ado let's begin this walk together on the road to not only understanding ourselves but also to understand how "our selves" many times causes people to question "themselves." When this happens, it prompts their actions. It's hard many times to realize that your aura, gifts, and shine can ultimately put others in an uncomfortable place and make them feel ill at ease. However, what you must remember is that it's not your issue and you cannot make their problems yours. We shall stop doing that from this point forward. Remember, through this journey of Self Re-Discovery (and say it with me) ...

"I AM worth the effort to take this journey. I AM worthy, more than worthy of the rewards, accolades, promotions, love, care, and attention that lie at the end of this journey."

Despite what anyone, anywhere says, thinks or believes, this is your shot; no one else's. You only get one shot at this life, make it count for you and not for anyone else.

I am not going to make any promises that this entire journey is going to be easy, but it will be worth it. I'm not going to say that there will not be things that will make you nervous to even try but try them anyway. Just keep in mind that for newness to happen, new things need to replace your old ways of doing things and your old thought processes. It's akin to CBT or Cognitive Behavioral Therapy. Look it up!

Our minds and brains control a lot of what we do, think, feel, and perceive. No one has the complete and utter control over it except you. It's like when you don't want to hear a song, you change the station. If you don't want to hear the negative, the hurt, and the inaccurate descriptions that people put on you, then turn it (and them) off. Turn the station and don't feel sorry for it. Then, replace that old station with a new, upbeat, positive station that delivers the nourishment you need to quench your palette.

Many times, people don't know how to love us because we don't know how to truly love ourselves correctly. We must let people see the blueprint to know how to follow it. However, to be able to supply a blueprint, we first must know what we are trying to build. We can't just hand people a blank sheet and say draw upon it what you feel I should have or what you feel I need. When we do that, we end up with proverbial houses that are only suitable for those on the outside to inhabit. There is no room for us or anyplace within that proverbial home that feels like our own. It's not custom-made to your specifications. Don't be afraid to build your blueprint then gift those in your life with the path to the yellow brick road. If they still decide to veer off, it is your responsibility to allow them to exit stage left.

People will deposit in your bank of life what you allow them to and if they keep withdrawing, ultimately you will be depleted. I know we've all heard something along those lines, but it bears repeating because it is common sense. Even if we hear it many times, we may still find it hard to comprehend such a simple phrase.

So again, I ask, are you ready? If so, take my hand for you will not do this alone. Let me pick you up from that darkness for I am a miner of diamonds. Just imagine the light on my helmet. :)

In the first three chapters, I will help you travel down memory lane. I will also open up about the trials and tribulations during those times of the chapters that led to my destruction, deconstruction, and my final reconstruction. The things that I will write are not meant for sympathy but are meant for transparency. In order to know where you are or where you have been, I want you to know that I have been there myself. It is essential to remember and understand what happened in the developmental years to understand what is needed for your deconstruction. Get ready to work!

Chapter 2
In The Very Beginning....

"Children Learn What They Live"

Dorothy Law Nolte

If children live with Criticism, they learn to Condemn.

If Children live with Hostility, they learn to Fight.

If Children live with Ridicule, they learn to be Shy.

If Children live with Shame, they learn to feel Guilty.

If children live with Encouragement, they learn Confidence.

If children live with Tolerance, they learn to be Patient.

If children live with Praise, they learn to Appreciate.

If children live with Acceptance, they learn to Love.

If children live with Approval, they learn to like Themselves.

If children live with Honesty, they learn Truthfulness.

If children live with Security, they learn to have Faith.

If children live with Friendliness, they learn the World is a nice place to live.

Ahhh, to be young again. We all have heard that saying so many times as we reminisce about the "good old days". We all have had those times when we recline and begin to pick the fond memories of school, family gatherings, summer camp, that old uncle who drank too much and always started a ruckus, or about the smell of cookies, pies, cakes baking and how the sunshine felt different on your skin back then. Reminiscing about making pillow forts and dreaming about being old enough, adult enough to do the "fun things" adults do.

I remember growing up I would always say, "When I am old enough, I am going to party and dance all night long with my friends!" I would daydream about how I was going to buy anything I wanted, how I was going to live in a penthouse in Manhattan and be fabulous all day, every day. I know I am not the only one who had those grandiose ideas about adulthood. Yes, we all thought being adults would be so much easier than being children and we also delighted in the fact that adults had no bedtime! Now that we are adults it's funny we think and dream all day about our bedtime, but when we were younger, it was like a life sentence.

While we are reminiscing about our childhood and teen years, what we often fail to realize is the adults of today were molded by the children of yesteryear and what we choose to remember at times fails to explain, describe or speak to the situations, encounters, adventures or misadventures and detrimental situations that growing up imparted to us. Some of those dark times play a major role in how as children we develop into young adults.

My Story....

Although I have fond memories of being a child, there were situations that happened which are difficult to speak about still to this day. Incidents and situations that have left scars that were untreated for years. My mother worked and was very involved with mine and my brother's life. And even at a young age, I realized how much she had on her plate. So, with that, I kept many things to myself. All I wanted for her and my brother was happiness, peace, joy, food to eat and lights on in the house. When you are a very attentive child as I was, you pay attention to cues given off by those you love. I watched my mom do whatever she needed to do to make sure we were safe and well taken care of. I didn't want to cause any trouble or add any stress she may have gone through. So, my thought process was easy. If I could just stay out-of-the-way and not cause trouble, then I would gladly take anything that came to me. Even at the young age of five, I learned to be quiet.

The first time I can recall making the decision to be quiet was about a situation with our babysitter's grandson. I recall him being very mean to me in front of his grandmother and adults, but as soon as she left the room or left him in charge of me, he wanted to play, "Married." I remember asking him what that meant, and he told me that he can do whatever he wanted to do to me. My job was to be the wife and to let him do what he wanted to do. He was about 13 years old and I hated when he would punch me or taunt me in ways that made me cry but I felt I had no choice. I remember crying every time the babysitter would leave him alone with me. I also remember trying to tell her what he was doing but I was shooed away because she didn't want to hear it. I was told to be quiet and to be a good girl. That was the beginning for me but not the end. At the age of 13, I had to revisit this scenario but with very real situations and circumstances. So many of these situations culminated to the night I wanted to end it all. Being a child isn't always easy.

We are told as children who we are, whom we should aspire to be, what to look like, what not to look like, who to emulate, what traits are good and bad, what to leave within and what to show. We are told how much to eat or not eat, how your sister or brother, cousin or best friend is "better than you" in some way. How if you only "do it our way" or "see it our way" you would be so much better off. We had no say in it at all and as our heads would spin around and around trying not to miss the "wisdom" being given, we were, in essence, beginning to build not who we were or might have wanted to be, but who we were told to be for after all, what did you know... you were just a mere child.

Please do not misunderstand me. I wholeheartedly believe that it is a parent's job to set a good example for their children. To guide them in a way that is positive and safe. I do believe in rules and regulations and consequences. It is our parent's job to raise us and to mold us. I believe a parent is a child's first example of how to be a well-adjusted adult. It is their job to pour into us as children all that they know. However, it is also important for us as parents to know how to pour into our children, what we are to pour into them and at what time are we to pour in certain ingredients. This is important because all children are not the same. We, as parents have the responsibility in monitoring the strength and dosage of our pouring in or imparting of the knowledge, circumstances, and situations that have helped to build, mold and guide us as children so that we can later teach our own children.

Simply put... it has a lot to do with the delivery. Think of it this way, all cars need gasoline and we must supply it for the car to run and get us to our destinations. However, even though all cars need gasoline to move, they all don't take the same grade of gasoline, hold the same amount of gasoline within their tanks, nor do they use gasoline in the same way. Now we have smart electronic cars that don't use gasoline at all. The underlying and related fact is that whether the car runs by gasoline or electricity, it needs something to help it move forward.

Simply put, in comparison to children there must be knowledge, love, lessons, morals, values and the like poured into them for them to move forward in their life's journey. Depending on the age of your child, the amount that you pour into them must be measured as well as the contents that is being delivered to different ages. The knowledge given is utilized differently depending on a child's age. As a child grows, so does all that is being deposited into them. However, if nothing good goes in, then nothing good will come out. I hope that makes sense. Right now many of us are sputtering, sluggish, broken cars that are in dire need of a tune-up and repairs. We are in need of upgrading our "gasoline" because of the low-grade that we have poured into our souls and spirits is no longer serving its purpose.

As young children we are told not to question our elders and to "do as I say, not as I do" so we take it all in as law and before we even realize it, it begins to mold us. It begins to formulate an internal paintbrush that we ultimately use to begin painting the landscape of our lives with the paints given. Some areas of the picture being painted may look beautiful, idyllic, but what happens when you just so happened to look at the top right corner. You know, up there where no one else is focusing? That spot in the painting where no one takes the time to recognize could be where all the beauty is focused. Ask yourself when you think about this area of the painting or the area of your life; is it blank or devoid of color? Or are the colors violent, disturbing, full of gashes and jagged lines? Or are there just two colors; black and white?

Even if others don't pay attention to them or to that place, we must realize they still exist. They all still matter. Those colors, that area of your personal landscape or painting still plays a part in the coming together or the construction of that picture. Realize that portrait is you.

You become comfortable with it being there and as a child, when that space is noticed or seeps out, those in charge of us would try to explain it away and give the answer to those on the outside looking in, "Oh, he/she is just that way" or "We are trying to get that attitude, attribute, habit, sadness out of them." Some were even sent to military schools because "The discipline will do them good!"

Although the thought was good, and the direction may have been needed, in many instances going to the extreme as mentioned above was not the answer. I've found that as children grow, their behaviors and ideas grow along with them. As such when they are met with the extreme in terms of dealing with trying to figure out their feelings, actions, and perceptions to many of life's daily issues, it leaves many feelings confused and their perceived course of action is in some way wrong and needs to be purged from their bodies and from their systems.

As children, our ideas and notions of what life is all about can be far-reaching but have merit and should never be dismissed. I am all for tweaking for safety or positive redirection to further enhance growth, but what a child expresses or is interested in should never be dismissed or replaced. In our quest to save our children, we many times erase who and what it is they are or want to become. Now don't get me wrong... If a child were intrigued with jumping into volcanoes, then maybe that idea should be examined and structured so he or she can possibly become the leading scientist who studies volcanoes. But let's also remember there is nothing wrong with a little girl architect or even aspiring to be the first female president. Let's not kill the dreams of the innocent.

In my travels of speaking with adults who are disenchanted with how their lives and careers have taken shape, they often revert to childhood when they were told that their ideas and dreams were silly and could never become their reality. It pains me to know this and for a while, I believed it myself. But just as I am pouring into you, I had to pour into myself and realize that if I wanted to become anything in this world, I had to shake off my fears and put one foot in front of the other and realize that I am worth the struggle. I had to not be afraid so that one day I would be able to emerge from my cocoon as a beautiful butterfly. Even when I was being told that I was nothing more than a failure, I had to dig down deep inside to realize that wasn't true. Many of those thoughts and feelings came from my childhood.

When we are children, we are told to trust those in power, those over us, those who are our caregivers without question. If that job is left up to those who either are broken within themselves or do not have our best interest at heart, it can lead to the beginning of the steps to the deconstruction of the authentic you. We don't see it but the childhood "us" evolves into the teenaged "us" who, along with all the hells of being a teenager, develops into the adult "us". How we perceive ourselves and the world around us, go after goals, stand up for ourselves, take part in the relationships we get into and the choices we ultimately make during our adult lives stem from and is related to the "YOU" of your childhood and teenage years. Our first intimate attachments in our teen years develop from how we attached ourselves as infants and young children.

The theory of attachment pertains to the ways in which infants develop bonds with those caregivers with whom the child comes in contact (Ainsworth & Bowlby, 1991). Depending on how this attachment is formed plays an important and crucial role in how an individual forms lasting bonds with those outside of the scope of their family and relatives. As a child your first experience with learning how to formulate and secure bonds and relationships start at home, stemming from whatever the child experiences in the way of home life and their family dynamics. What we need to understand is that the home life begins the process of determining the group of attachment through which we as infants develop. As such, these experiences not only affect us in infancy but has also been discovered that it impacts relationship formation in later years (Hendricks et al, 2005; Madison, 2010; Williams,2004).

In his research, Bowlby felt that there was a link that existed between the ways children attached to their caregivers and later the ways they attached romantically to partners later in life (Brehem et al, 2005). In research done by Arbona and Power (2003) they defined attachment as a strong bond that grows between an infant and their primary caregiver that is supportive and encouraging. The foundation that is built by this bond will become the foundation from which the child or we as children begin to progress into other personal and interpersonal relationships beyond that of our primary caregivers (Arbona & Power,2003; Morton, 2006). The internalized working models of the attachment-related experiences help us to form our sense of worthiness, which later interferes with responsiveness to others and affect emotional adjustment and social competency later in life which also plays a part in developing self-esteem (Arbona &Power, 2003).

With that tidbit of information, it is very important to watch what we pour into our children as well as what was poured into us as we grew and developed. Broken children, sad children, negatively attached, neglected children, children who were told they were less than, those who were passed over, bullied children, scared children, nervous children, and stifled children many times can become those same adults if discovery and growth are stunted at those phases, crucial situations and areas of life. Many times, unbeknownst to ourselves we carry those things into our adult lives and as we continue to grow and mature they become deeply ingrained in us to where they now become our ways of life and our habits we engage in daily. Those ways of being, even the slightest adoption of the elements of what was poured into us become our calling card and our second nature. Then by the time, we realize we want to make a change we feel lost and alone because for so long we operated from the standpoint of what we brought from our attachments and our childhood. So, if you had a dramatic, catastrophic, hurtful, disappointing, made to feel less than the type of situations that happened to you in your childhood, there is a great possibility that manifestation will appear in your adult life.

Even if those things happen, we must keep in mind that all is not lost. You are here, and you are breathing so you can change the way you think, feel, and perceive things. As soon as you recognize that you are carrying this unnecessary, heavy, burdensome way of being, you can actively take the steps to become who and what you really are and want to become. All is not lost. It doesn't matter the age or the situation or circumstance.

You can always take your negatives and turn them into positives. Just because you used to be this or that does not mean you necessarily have to continue to be that. Do you understand what I'm saying to you? Out with the old and in with the new. Take hopeful solace in the fact that all is not lost, and it is not too late to rebuild. The first step is to acknowledge what these things are and then work on them.

Just as you give your all to everyone on the outside, let's first recognize that giving yourself that type of love and attention is necessary. Just as you feel that everyone on the outside is worth it, realize *you* are worth it! Just as you give all that time, attention and effortless work to better the lives of everyone else around you to make them happy, you must realize that *you* are worthy of the work as well! Your past does not define your future unless you stay stagnant.

HOMEWORK TIME!!!

Before you can fix what is broken you must first know what's broken. So now is the time for our first honesty check. Take time out, alone time and get a journal. One thing you will have to remember is through this journey you will be doing a lot of chronic holding and journaling. Think about your childhood. Think about and write down the fond memories. These will be those memories that bring the sunshine to our spirits. These will be memories that we will revisit and some we will save. After you are finished with the sunshine, we will have to encounter some rain. You must have one in order to appreciate the other. You will now enter your stormy season. It is now time to chronicle those times of hurt, pain, shame, loneliness, confusion. Pay attention to all the words or phrases that come up with in you from your walk down memory lane. These phrases can be actual phrases or can be your own perceptions that arise from situations you endured growing up. Feel them. It's okay to cry, get angry or feel confused. It's a purge so you must feel it. Let it all sit with you. Many times, these are the parts of our lives that we try to forget, but what we don't fully grasp is that although we are not trying to consciously recall them, they still subconsciously play a part in how we maneuver in many parts of our lives.

After you've finished chronicling all these things I need you to look at your list. It is now your time to pay attention to this terrible list. Look at what you've written down and truly be honest with yourself. Which one of these things are totally untrue? Which one of these things is a label that someone placed on you and unbeknownst to yourself adopted the definition of that label or labels? Which one of these things on this list are things that you want to do away with forever because you know they are holding you back? When you see it, which one of these things brings a sad, dark feeling that overtakes your soul? Again, sit with all these things and have discussions within yourself. There is no need to call anyone to ask them if these things are true because at this moment you are beginning your journey of reconstruction. For the first time probably in a long time this is all about you.

After you have finished taking stock of your list, it is now time for the next phase. Tear the list out of your journal and fold the paper in fours. Make it into an origami swan, ball it up so that it is closed. It is now time to physically watch this list get its just desserts.

Get some matches and go where you can safely light those horrible things that were said or happened to you on fire. Once you are in a safe spot, lay the paper down and be prepared to say goodbye to all those horrible, untrue things, perceptions, feelings, and situations that may have become true in one way or another within your life. Let your tears be like lighter fluid. Then as you look at the paper that is laid before you folded neatly or crumbled up however you did it, set it on fire! Yes! Burn it to complete nothingness. As it burns into ashes and is carried away by the wind, visualize those feelings within you floating away. They are disintegrating into the nothingness. Just like the paper you are going through a transformation and will never be the same.

You will never revert to what you once were or who you once were. You will no longer be what they said about you and what you put on that paper. Let your tears cleanse you. Don't feel ashamed about your reactions to what you've just done. Many of us for as long as we can remember have done things or neglected to do things because of how we felt others would view us or what they told us our reactions represented. You are no longer living that way. Now take a few more minutes and let it out. This is only the beginning... we still have work to do.

"We delight in the beauty of the butterfly, but rarely admit the changes it has gone through to achieve that beauty"

~ Maya Angelou

Now take a deep sigh of relief and get up. Wipe your face and notice how it feels to walk in your glory, in your own beautiful, purposeful, unique, and authentic shine. Come on, get used to it just like you got used to the baggage, the labels, and definitions others used to describe you. Now it's time for you to get used to all of what you truly represent. If it's so easy to adopt the negative, let's try to change that and adopt the positive. This is the beginning of the end of the old you at the beginning of the reconstruction of the new you. Think of it this way... you are like a butterfly, but before you can spread your wings and fly you must retreat into your chrysalis. What we are going to do is make your chrysalis, your cocoon comfortable for you because soon you are going to emerge as this dynamic, colorful, full of life, magical, one-of-a-kind butterfly. The type of butterfly that does not need the recognition of others for you have been recognized by the one person who has the power, and the authority to make or break you! The one person who holds your happiness, growth, and development in their hands. That person is YOU.

"Just when the caterpillar thought the world was over, it

became a butterfly."

I can see it, can you? If you can't right now, it's okay. You just must keep going until your vision becomes clearer. This transformational metamorphosis is not going to happen overnight. It took years to build you into the person that you are now, so it will take time and effort to get you deconstructed and through your reconstruction. Each step no matter how small is a step in the right direction. It does not keep you stagnant and that is a word that we are going to hear often because that is a word that we do not want to bring into your reconstruction process. I once heard that if you want something, do not rush it because you do not want to rush things that you want to last forever. So, breathe deep and let's get to our next chapter.

YOU ARE POWERFUL!

Chapter 3
Your Next Phase- Adolescence

"Adolescence represents an inner emotional upheaval, a struggle between the eternal human wish to cling to the past and the equally powerful wish to get on with the future."

~ Louise J. Kaplan

Does he like me? Should I ask her out? Why is my faith always under attack? Am I too fat? Am I straight? Am I gay? Will I be accepted? Am I popular? Why am I not popular? Should I do "it" just because "they" are doing it? Will I get into a good college? What will I be when I grow up? Are my parents proud of me? Will I always be an outsider?... The list of questions, concerns, hormonal changes, friendship dynamics, fears about adult life, growth spurts or the lack thereof, divorces, miscommunications and the like are endless and continue as we progressed from the ages of 13 to 19. Consequently, the issues from the ages of 13 to 19 seem to continue and later formulate how we attack and deal with the myriad of issues that arise as we enter our 20s and beyond. Each age and new year acts as the building blocks for a new or deeper challenge that we must face.

This time in our development is difficult. Then, add in the likelihood of becoming involved in your first real intimate relationship and you have a recipe for outbursts, false ideas about who you are and who you are going to be as you progress in life. Your fantasies and dreams shattered from when you were just a young person with lights and stars in your eyes.

During this time life acceptance is huge. For many it becomes something that is craved and depending on the amount of acceptance received from peers and family, it becomes a motivating force behind many of our actions. Unfortunately, many times it may backfire to a person's own detriment. Your teenage or adolescent years are also a time where many gain more freedoms and responsibilities. From those freedoms and responsibilities, the lessons and experiences gathered from associated events become ingrained into how we develop and what perceptions, emotions, and ideas we bring into our adult lives.

We take all that we are, what we have been told and have endured and we identify with it all and the result is that we somehow make it represent "us". We claim it as the calling card for whom and what we represent to the world at large. What happens in our adolescence has a direct impact on our progression and it sets the stage for what happens down the line.

The term "Growing Pains" is an understatement for we are not only growing physically but also emotionally, consciously and subconsciously. What I mean by that is we don't recognize those little insipid things that attached to our brains that we give life to and allow to manifest. Before we realize it, we are doing, acting, thinking, and begin to perceive things in ways that sometimes cause us to ponder the questions, "Now where did that come from?" When did I begin to maneuver life this way?" Yes, the teen years. Those wonderful, wonderful teen years!

Now don't get me wrong, the purpose of this chapter wasn't to pick apart or sully the great, magical, exciting and nostalgic memories these years bring bubbling to the surface. I too remember my first dance, first date, first unchaperoned movie dates with friends, hell I even remember my first lover at the age of 16 during the parent-teacher convention week in November 1989 – 1990. He was a young man who would later become the first physically, mentally and emotionally abusive boyfriend I ever had in my life. Now I realize it was I who continued the cycle of abuse that I saw growing up unbeknownst to me at the time. In essence, I looked for what I grew up witnessing.

For I, both consciously and subconsciously, used to believe that if a man wasn't beating me, berating me or cheating on me then it was obvious that he did not love me at all. Love, at that time, was physical. It had to be felt even if blood had to be drawn. It showed "attention" being paid, time being spent, and "affection" being shown.

During my teen years love = pain, love = sex, love=unworthiness. It would be many years and many other forays into different types of abuse before I would grow to realize that love in action has healing properties. Love may cause tears, but constant tears are not a prerequisite for its activation. Tears cleanse, clears away stress, and is a welcomed signal to the feelings of many beautiful things that this life has to offer.

Well enough about me for now. Again in order for you to take this walk there has to be some trust built and through opening my life to you, in essence baring all, my hope is that you allow me to walk with you; not as the author of a book, but as a real person who has and still does endure the slings and arrows of life just like you. So onward and upward.

There are many times loving others, or the idea of loving others becomes so entrenched in our minds and spirits that we begin to forget and neglect ourselves. If you take a moment to think back to your adolescents, I am sure you will be able to recollect many times when this occurred. When you strived to become a part of the popular crowd. The crowd that everyone adored including teachers. The time when you were told that to be accepted, loved, noticed, dated and the like, it would be in your best interest to conform to the idea of what would bring such comfort to your life. When you were told that you had to change certain things about who you were, what you wanted, how you should feel, who and what you should aspire to be, what you should and should not look like and the list on and on, did you buy into it? And let's be realistic, looking at television and reading magazines solidified this way of thinking. Due to this developmental time in your life, those things had such a crucial effect on how you grow. During this time you are desperately trying to figure out where you belong and where you want to belong. We are, in essence trying to make our uncomfortable feelings into comfortable, cool and acceptable happiness. The quest for acceptance and assimilation is real!

(Just as a sidebar... This is totally off the subject in a way, but when we think back to those cool kids, the ones who were popular and destined for greatness, where are they now? Did that popularity serve them well into adulthood or did they to find that they were loving something so much that they lost themselves in the midst of it all and now they are using their adult lives to find themselves. Are you trying to live authentically? Just a thought).

During our adolescents, we are like thirsty plants. We need to be fed, pruned, nurtured and replanted for our ideal growth. However, just like the car analogy, the ingredients required for ideal growth must be of a higher grade to get the best out of the plant possible. Let's face it, as young adults we are thirsty. Thirsty for attention, acceptance and an identity. We are looking for answers to life's questions and we seek excitement and direction. So, imagine as we searched for all those things to quench our thirst, and satiate our appetites. However, what we were given and what we accepted got ingrained in our core.

Think about how life is cyclical and how what we were given we have in turn disseminated some or many of those things that may not have been the best ingredients to those in our sphere, in our charge and care. Unbeknownst to us many times the cycle of dysfunction, unhappiness, poor self-esteem, feeling lost and the like get passed down because we are only giving back what was given. What we adopted and accepted became our perceptions. Even when we make the concerted effort to "do differently what was done to us" we many times miss the mark because we are so hell-bent on doing the opposite to others of what has been done to us. When we do this, we fail to see that our "different" is just an extension of our "same". For we are allowing others to drink from the same dysfunctional, hurtful, disillusioned well that we thought we closed off and drained.

Although this may be a hurtful scenario to be a part of, there is one silver lining in it all. It's not too late to change for each day grants a new seed that can be planted. The only failure aside from recognizing things need to change is sitting idly by and doing nothing. Change is a word that suggests action. So, what are you waiting for? It's time for a change.

Now here comes the educator in me giving you more homework! I promise not to give homework in every chapter, but it is important for your growth. Your homework is this... More Reflection. Think back to your teenage years. Think about your ambitions at that time. What was one thing, at least one thing, that you wanted to accomplish, and you did when you became an adult? Really think hard. What was it? How did you accomplish it? How did it feel?

Now do the opposite. Think of one thing that you wanted to accomplish but didn't. Ask yourself truthfully why it was not accomplished. What happened? What stopped you? Do you use those same self-defeating actions to stunt your growth in other areas currently? Where did those ideas or ways of thinking stem from? Who did they stem from? Now think about that person and how their life turned out?

In reflecting on those who poured the negative into our lives and then witnessing their lives now, it gives you a more complete picture and reference point. It helps you in realizing that they too may not have been aware of the unhealthy ingredients they were spewing and pouring into your life because, more often than not, they were also being fed the same diet. If they are still trying to tell you how to live your life and what would be best for you and their lives are far from the perfect path they are trying to have you walk, then you will realize that those are not the people to which you should listen. Here's an analogy: if you want to get your hair done in a beautiful style, why would you go to a salon where the beautician's hair is unhealthy and broken off? How could that stylist guide you in how to keep your hair healthy? How can he/she make you look presentable and beautiful if he/she cannot do it for themselves?

Another analogy: if you were suffering from a disease or an illness and you needed to go to a specialist, would you seek out a doctor or specialist who themselves was sick and suffering from illnesses that they claim to be able to cure? EXACTLY! No, you wouldn't. Apply that same analogy to those in your life who are trying to lead you, but who cannot lead themselves.

Take your time with this homework. I want you to really sit and reflect and feel these flashbacks. You need to commit these feelings and times into your mind so that you will know what to change, what to take out and replace when you begin your reconstruction.

Chapter 4

Adulting: It's Myths and Realities

"Most people don't grow up. Most people age. They find parking spaces, honor their credit cards, get married, have children, and call that maturity. What that is, is aging."

~Maya Angelou

The Myths

Think back to your 21st birthday. Think about all the anticipation that led up to that day! The plans, the party, the outfit, the staying out all night, the legal drinking. Ahhhh yes, you get to do all the things that in your youthful days you envisioned adults got to do. In your mind you have finally arrived! Do you remember how you felt? The sun was shining brighter, the nights were all your own for there was finally no bedtime. Your conversations were going to become more adult. You adopted the mindset of, "I need my coffee in the morning in order for my day to start on the right foot." You got to complain about rush hour traffic and one of the biggest achievements is that you did not have to check the box on surveys or questionnaires that stated the age range from 15 to 20. Now you are 21! With this new achievement or rank in age you are now officially able to say with all pride and privileges, "I am a grown ass man\woman and I can do whatever the hell I want!" Honestly who was going to debate that fact? This is the holy grail of adult statements.

In our years leading up to our 21st birthday we all thought that once we hit adulthood everything would be easier. We would have no rules and, in our minds, having no rules meant that we could either make them up as we went along, or we were able to be as free as birds because there was nothing to hold us back. We thought that the freedom of adulthood would last forever. When we saw our parents without that beautiful smile that should accompany adulthood many times we thought that they were just overreacting. Honestly, did they not know how unbelievably well they had it? When we hit that magical age of 21, we envisioned as each year progressed things could only get better. After all, as each year passes you would be growing deeper into your freedom. Oh, how very wrong we were to ever have those delusions of grandeur for we would soon find that this stage in life is even more difficult than childhood.

The Realities

Now I'm not a betting woman, but if I were, I believe I can guess what your favorite turn of phrase is at this moment... "Man, if I could just go back to when I was a kid! Life was so much simpler then." Being that we were in such a hurry to "get grown" it now feels as if we've rushed past the times that now, looking back, were for all tense and purposes, the most carefree, innocent, stress-free, joyful times we will ever experience. Many of us had everything done for and handed to us. Now sometimes we feel so stupid for complaining about having to do such things as the dishes. How the teenaged heartaches and breakups pale in comparison to the divorces and endings we endure now. How we thought that being able to drive a car meant freedom, but really with payments, insurance, repairs and the like it's more of a hindrance and money vacuum than anything else. How when we thought staying up late was the greatest thing ever, but now if we aren't in bed by 10PM, we are messed up for the next day's shuttle runs in getting the kids to school or getting to work on time ourselves.

Now, I'm not saying that being an adult does not have its advantages and bright spots, but let's face it, it's not how we conjured it up to be. It's true, hindsight is 20/20 for if I knew then as a child what I know now, I really would have cherished those days of old. Those times when I thought we had won the lottery because my mom was able to treat my brother and I to cheeseburgers from Burger King or when I had to go to sleep early on Christmas Eve so that Santa Claus could sneak down my chimney and only give me half of what I asked for on my list. The wonderment I felt trying to figure out how this man who sees all and knows all managed to get into my chimneyless, fireplace-less house without waking any of us as he carried his bag of toys into my tiny living quarters. Now, the tale sounds like a stalker-ish nightmare, but you get my point.

Instead now I am diligently working to afford my daughter the life full of memories, experiences, playdates, sports lessons, good schools, healthcare and such that I either had or wished so desperately to have had. My childhood is another book entirely. It will make you cry, laugh, say, "what the hell" and cheer before you reached the back cover. But again, this book is about and for you. Let's stick to and dissect your times currently, what we see, feel and are destined to change for this again is the beginning of your metamorphosis. Right now, you are resting in your Cocoon of Consciousness. You must rest up in order to bring out the best that lies within.

I see you striving every day. You juggle many balls in the air and many times before a thankless crowd. You juggle work, children, healthcare, the elderly or sick parents and children, rent, mortgage, weight loss, weight gain, unrest in society, your personal safety, employment, unemployment or underemployment, failed relationships, estrangement, being passed over for promotions, paying bills, hurts from the past that affect your present, self -discovery, rumors, haters, naysayers, requests and infringements on your time and regrets for things that you have not done. There are many things that I may have failed to mention that should have also made the list, but the fact remains that you do all of this within the 24 hours given within each day. I am willing to bet that even when you sleep, your rest is disturbed because your mind is restless. No matter how hard you try or how many melatonin you consume, it will not shut off. So right now, you, me, we are going to actively, consciously, bravely look at all you do and all you endure. Instead of looking at your weaknesses, we will focus on how powerful you really are.

I want you to begin to consciously look at how you are the glue that keeps so many things together. How, without you, lunches would not be made, work would not get done, love wouldn't be given, boo boos would go unkissed, deadlines wouldn't get met, how many times your shoulder would go un-cried on and the list goes on and on. But now it's time to incorporate a word that many of us have a hard time saying; that word is 'NO'. Many times, unbeknownst to us, we are all things to all people because in all those pieces we keep together we find our worth. Many times it also keeps us from giving to ourselves and it keeps us from really having to feel and face our own issues, situations, hurts, pains and places where improvements are needed.

We get our worth from hearing and feeling we are in fact worthy in the eyes of others. However, this book was written to help you to recognize you are worthy and the worth starts with you realizing your self-worth.

So now you are going to actively say the word "STOP!" We are going to have to make this world-wind of a day-to-day activity sheet stop. You are going to learn to incorporate reflection time. I want you to not feel guilty about giving yourself a moment to relax and breathe. Now we are not going to stop forever, but for a few minutes, right now, you must. Hopefully this practice will become an important part of your life. Call it your "Me Moment." You are going to learn how to acknowledge unabashedly your greatness.

Come on, sit right down in your comfy chair or stand in your shower and think about you! Look at all you do! Look at all you accomplish on a daily basis. Now take your hand and pat yourself on the back. Heck, even chant your own name or give yourself an amazing speech. Understand that in order to begin the journey to fixing what is broken, it will help you to realize that you are not all bad. I want you to realize that you have the power to endure many things and that the keys of change lie within your reach. If you can affect goodness within the lives of those you love then you are damn sure capable of giving back that same care, concern, energy and acknowledgment to the person who makes it happen for everyone else. That person is you!

Many times, a key component in how we handle ourselves and why we seem to abandon ourselves is that we neglect to become and fall in love with ourselves. We are so eager to be attached and to be in love with others hoping that they will make us complete when in all actuality the first person we should be in love with and do for is ourselves.

You are, whether you know it or not, the greatest gift to yourself. You are the person who has the great privilege of waking up with and to you every day. You have the great privilege of pampering yourself, feeding your physical as well as your emotional and spiritual well-being. You are the person that knows your deepest fears, passions and ambitions. All the things that you encompass can be an asset to your very core just as it is an asset to those around you. Realize that no one knows you better than you know yourself. But as it is in human nature, we usually neglect and shortchange the ones we are closest to. We ignore and deprive ourselves of the barest of essentials while we pour out those same gems and jewels to others.

We do this because we always think that we can come back and save ourselves at a later date. And the more we do that, the love affair that we are supposed to be building within takes a backseat to the love affairs and connections we make with those outside of who we are. We look at and allow them, their needs, their wants, their happiness as well as their sadness to takes center stage while we settle away comfortably in the backseat…. fading to black. Many times these things happen without our realizing it or even wanting it to manifest. All we notice is that for some reason we are losing our zest for life.

We begin to realize that we are zapped of energy and the things that used to once bring us joy, we either do very little or nothing at all.

We began to log the days as just time and not as moments in time. We become depressed and begin to replace our natural highs with artificial ones. This way of life can go on for years. We become comfortable with allowing this dull light to be the only illumination from which we see ourselves. In dim, dull light we see things in our lives in the same way; dim, dull, dark and lifeless. Although we know we were put here to connect with others, to procreate and fall in love, to leave our mark, nowhere in the playbook did it say lose yourself within the process. There are many ways and scenarios that make it easy for us, especially women to lose track and focus of who we are and the greatness we possess.

Many times we fall out of love with ourselves because we are too busy comparing where we are to the progress and station of others. We use those metrics to measure our own success. We look at what others are doing and at what age they are doing it and if we are behind them in some way, we feel as if we are not worthy to continue the race to get where we want to go. We begin to adopt the outside definitions of what someone in our "perceived place" would be called and we adopt those said definitions for ourselves. We need to realize that during all of this, everyone's road is different and with that being the case we must embrace the road that we are on and do our due diligence to make it as smooth a passage as we can. Who is going to give you everything in this life that you want? The answer is simple; You! We need to worry about the idea of loving ourselves instead of the idea of other people loving us. Many times we lose ourselves trying to find someone else.

I am not saying that having someone in your life is in some way going to hinder your progress, but if the only time you see your greatness is when others are the catalyst for it and that is what causes you to move differently and perceive differently, then you are doing yourself a disservice.

It is true that when those we love see us and cast us in a beautiful and warm light, our confidence soars. When we are acknowledged, we are apt to engage with others more and go after what we want with greater zeal. But shouldn't we be able to make ourselves feel just as invincible? In essence shouldn't we have that same regard for how we view ourselves as we have when others outside of us pay us attention? It's easy to feed off the good vibes of others and yet harder to find those same vibes to feed our own hunger when we must dig deep in order to tap into it.

We must realize that how we feel or view ourselves is connected to the positive regard of someone else's accolades. It in fact is how we filter those words through our minds that we assign our personal level of greatness. Depending on the level of importance we place on the individual supplying those words being lavished upon us, the greater it impacts how we feel about ourselves. So, then the question becomes if our perceived importance and greatness that we see through the eyes of another can cause such euphoria, then why can't we through the same self-love cause the same reactions when we decide to love ourselves?

Think about it; even those who we swore would love us forever, would have our best interest at heart, the ones we gave our bodies and souls too, many times leave and with them they take all those wonderful things we built up about ourselves through their approval and our interaction with them. When this happens, it leaves us fully alone and lost. We feel less of who we once were. However, we must then ask ourselves how we can find a way to ultimately keep these feelings, perceptions, visions, self-worth and the like within us no matter what life brings our way. The answer is by being in love with ourselves. By being that lover that never leaves. By building foundations within ourselves and for ourselves that cannot, at a whim be taken away by others. Remember what was not supplied by others cannot be taken away by others.

Some of us have been so torn down that we don't know where to start in order to begin to fall in love with or make love to ourselves. We see ourselves as an unlovable mess. Someone took our kindness for weakness, played us, told us what we wanted to hear while we knew better and saw the truth. We allowed ourselves to be used while we were lonely, and the list goes on and on. We feel unworthy of love which causes us to neglect to love ourselves. In this time it is so hard to realize that we have so much love to give and not just to those on the outside. We find it so hard to turn that love inward because we are so used to finding our validation and self-worth and love from what others supply. Many times, this is the only way we know how to accept love.

Now it's time to stop.

Right now I'm going to give you some ways to begin to learn to lavish yourself with love and kindness. I want to teach you how to accept the love of self. We will take baby steps however; the goal is to take steps. One thing you can do is to sit with yourself for a while. I know that may sound simple, but rarely do we make a conscious effort to sit and acknowledge our presence. Learn to love your own company. Learn to quiet your mind, body and soul to realize that you don't always have to be on the go to feel as if you are doing right by the world at large.

Take yourself out to eat! Pamper yourself – you are worth it. Many times, we look upon pampering ourselves as selfish. We are constantly told this. However, if you are always being selfless with others, then why consider it selfish to recharge the batteries from within that being selfless depletes? Look at it this way... being selfless and selfish are mutually exclusive and as such are considered opposites. So, you cannot have both at the same time. What I'm trying to say is if you are selfless all the time, taking time to recharge is not a selfish act at all. If it helps to look at it this way, you must be selfish sometimes in order to continue to be selfless for others.

Another thing you can do is stop being so gullible and available to those on the outside that hurt you. That is self-explanatory for when we allow others to hurt us they then dim our light and ultimately deplete us of the energies that we could have stored and used to give love to ourselves.

Remember people can only do to you what you allow them to do. So, if you want it to stop then be the force that causes all the hurt to stop. Some people are not made to go with you on every journey or at every level of your life. It is okay to say no and it is okay to walk away.

Something else you can try... write down the good qualities about yourself that make you exceptional. When people try to tell you who you are, don't believe that BS. If it doesn't resonate with you or it makes you feel less than the extraordinary person you are, then trash it. You are more than capable of finding out all you encompass for yourself. Learn to believe in what you see before you instead of what those before you are trying to have you see. We have all been granted two eyes and some of us are privileged enough to know how to use our third eye; so, use them. You must also realize that you have a set of gifts that no one else has. Let go of the past hurts hurtful words and mistakes that you may have made. Know that your past does not define who you are presently and who you will be in the future. Stop doing what you've done so you can stop getting what you always get. Know that there is more to you than what you've been told.

The word or title "adult" should not bring up visions of baggy eyes, hardships, nagging bosses, empty pockets, thinning hair and expanding waistlines. It should be a time of experiencing life through the lenses and passions that we are capable of supplying for ourselves. Many times, we look at all that's wrong in our lives and wonder why things never seem to change. Could it be due to what you feel or think? Could it be how we attack those situations when they arise? Could it be the relationships we settled for and stay in? Could it be our fear of change? Whatever it is the one underlying fact is the same across the board; we have the power and control to change it all!

Like the saying goes the definition of insanity is doing the same thing over and over and expecting a different result. So that's our mission. Let's not continue to make ourselves insane by continuing to do the same things that we've done in the past which have yielded the results that we find ourselves in now. Let's overwhelmingly surprise ourselves with all we could do and all we can change when we start to bet on and believe in ourselves. Be a now person! Look at yourself as you view others. The cape that you used to put on to run to the rescue of others will now be used to save yourself.

Find Your Theme Music

We all have certain songs that we hear that touch us deeply in our spirit. Songs that make us feel alive and capable. Some of the songs bring back memories while other songs are making new memories. Your assignment is to think about a song that hits you right in your chest. That song that motivates you to jump up and get things done. The one that causes you to view yourself as invincible or at the very least a song that makes you happy. This song is a personal song and does not have to pass the approval of anyone in your circle of friends or family. You can play this song and it is not necessary to give anyone an explanation about why you are playing a particular song. Again, this reconstruction is about you and as such we are going to limit the times where we seek approval or replay in our minds what we feel those people that we surround ourselves with will say. Whatever song it is, it's the right song for you.

After you have selected the perfect song that makes your heart sing, it is now time to label that as your theme song. This is the song that is going to be synonymous with happiness, joy, fortitude, success, positivity, leveling up, new horizons and most importantly your reconstruction. You must play the song at least once every other day, if not every day and always when you need a lift. Also, play it when you "Save the Day" of those in your charge or even when you save the day for yourself. Play it to recharge your batteries and as your battle cry! Go ahead, Superhero... Go get your song!

Chapter 5

Rewriting Your Manifesto... Let's Get To Work

"We all have two lives. The second starts when we realize we only have ONE"

~ Tom Hiddleston

Now that you have walked down memory lane, it is time to take all that you revisited and raised from the recesses of your mind to use it to plot the course for your comeback! It is time to begin your reconstruction. It is now time to get to work in rewriting the script that you have lived and have been given by others. It's time to write your manifesto. I, whether you know it or not, am fully committed to your fight, as well as your road to redemption and reconstruction. This magnificent journey isn't one that I take lightly. You will come out of the darkness and into your personal, blinding, amazing light. What I need you to realize is that you matter. You matter not only to me, but it is time for you to matter to yourself. The greatness that is locked within your spirit is something this world needs. So, before you go back to making personal sacrifices and deposits to the world, you must deliver that greatness to yourself. No one can walk in your destiny quite like you and you've wasted enough time living in the shadows. It's now time to live fearlessly out loud. The only limitations you have are the ones in which you set in place for yourself.

Whether picked up from others or self-imposed, you have consciously and unconsciously lived the scripts and embodied the being of the elements that you allowed to stick to you from others. So just as easily as it was and is to allow the negative, meek, unflattering, hurtful, untrue, production–stopping, barrier creating thoughts, adjectives, perceptions and actions to stick to you and navigate your life, you can actively and on purpose adopt and believe the converse. You now have the power to adopt and believe the positive, true, amazing, barrier-breaking, flattery, loving, product–producing, self-worth building, perceptions, additives, and actions that you need to keep propelling you through this thing called life. For we only get one go around in our current form, so why not rock it until the wheels fall off? Why not shoot for the stars and attempt to shine among them? Anything worth having at all is worth the blood, sweat, and tears it takes to get it for the harder the work the deeper the appreciation you will have for and in yourself knowing that you did not stop.

It is now time for action. It is now time to get to work. The word "work" doesn't and shouldn't always suggest fear, being tired or even a quick fix. Through work lessons are learned and stamina is created. Through work, actions are executed, and progress is made. Through work, strength is built, and construction/reconstruction is completed. However, before work can begin plans need to be drawn up. To actively draw up the plans or blueprints, we must first have some idea about what we are trying to build. We must know what we want to manifest. As it relates to your reconstruction, your plan is simply creating your thoughts. To truly succeed with your plans, you must get rid of the idea that this reconstruction and manifestation you are undertaking is too big. You cannot focus on the fact that the new you may not meet the approval of others or that you feel you are not worthy. You must throw out the idea of saying to yourself "I don't have the time" or that you cannot afford it. Whatever negative ideas this fear of the new you may conjure up must be thrown to the wayside. Constantly remember that you are shooting for the stars.

Another way to look at this is through the eyes of a business deal. When in business you are often told to go above the asking price to get at least close to your bottom line. Many times, this tactic works. Depending on how believable and committed you are in negotiating the deal, some walk out of a deal with not only what they hoped to get, but with more than they asked for going into the deal. Do you know why that is? Simply put, the broker presented themselves in a light that showed him/her as deserving of it all. Think of yourself that way, "deserving of it all!" Even if they went into the negotiations nervous, shaky and unsure of their abilities, they did not show it.

So, step one – take the time to truly think about who you are and what you want to reconstruct. Think about what you want to manifest in your life. Read other people's stories you admire and see what their successful journeys look like. See how their dreams started off as tiny seeds within their souls that they had to plant, tend to, water, nurture, and weed in order for their dream seeds to crack open and bring forth the life that was inside of them. The life they call their own today. So, what is it going to be? What do you want to manifest? What is burning inside of you that you continually bury or "put off until the time is right?" One thing that you need to realize is that no time is ever completely right or opportune when it comes to undertaking situations, stepping out on faith, going after that new job or starting that new diet. There is never a 100% ideal time to undertake pretty much anything. The right time presents itself when you say enough is enough! It's when you decide to put one foot in front of the other and begin the process of moving towards turning your thoughts into verbalized words and your words into actions. Like the saying goes, "If you continue to persist, it is guaranteed that progress will happen." In other words, if you act on it, if you move and start the process, it is inevitable that you will begin to see results. Progress will be made, and something is going to happen because you are the force acting upon that which is your goals, dreams, and aspirations. The reconstruction of your life.

So now is the time to think about it. Ask yourself, "What do I really want?" Make the choice of either standing still or begin moving forward. Don't get discouraged. This reconstruction will be worth the time. Just remember Rome was not built in a day and this process of reconstruction can be repeated as you tackle different areas of your personal life. Just as Rome wasn't built in a day, remember, it was built! You must begin building your Rome.

With that being said now put this book down and think about what you are going to tackle first. Don't worry, I will wait. Go get your journal and write it down. Take the seed out of the case or envelope (the seed being a metaphor for your wants, thoughts, desires, goals, etc.) After that is done, come back to this page and let us continue to the next step. Don't cheat and don't read on! Don't rush! Just bookmark this page. You want this process to lead to your reality – your best life. It's the beginning of your new script, your manifesto. The subject is an important part of any written work. Aren't you worth taking time to get all you need and deserve? Yes, you are. Start writing...

Welcome back! The next step in your quest for reconstruction is now being able to take your idea/seed and start planting it so that your energy can begin to give it life. It has gone from just a mere fleeting thought to slow and deliberate action. You are putting one foot in front of the other catching momentum and making progress. So on to the next step, which may sound redundant, but it isn't because it is very necessary. Now you must sit and read your words over and visualize it! Whether you know it or not, this step is one that you will revisit often for it provides reinforcement, motivation, and excitement. It provides the push you need to continue towards where you want to be, where you are meant to be and where, with constant persistence, will become your new residence.

So, this time get a glass of wine, water, juice, champagne or whatever tickles your fancy and take in all the incredible and possible images your mind is depositing into your spirit. Take note of how you feel when you transport yourself into your new permanent space. Commit it to memory. Now lift your glass and sip in the good life. As you begin to deconstruct the old and reconstruct the new, the more detailed and intricate this new vision will become. Think of it this way, it's like building a house.

First, you have the preliminary idea of how and where you want your house to be built and how it is to look. Then it is on to sketching out the plans. You add, subtract and erase until you have a workable piece in front of you. Then you proofread the plans. You must make sure that it makes sense and that you will be comfortable living in your newly constructed dwelling. Then finally you begin to take steps to build the foundation. Once the foundation is laid, you then begin to build the rest of your dream home on that sturdy foundation. You will notice that after the house is built, there will be aspects that you would like to add or maybe take away. You may come to the realization that you have more to work with and your dwelling becomes more intricate and custom-made to fit your comfort. After your home is built, you move in! This becomes your new space. Right now, we are at the stage of admiring your work before we proofread the plans and begin to take the steps needed to make the paper plans come to life. You are going to make this a tangible dwelling. You will be comfortable in your own skin using your new wings to soar with the rest of the eagles.

Chapter 6

Making Your Reconstruction Manifesto Into Manageable Ideas

"The man who moves a mountain begins by carrying away small stones"

~Confucius

Time to get your hands dirty! It's time to make things easy and more manageable to reap the best harvests from this bumper crop of new life you are planting. Remember, little steps are still just that, steps. In order to move a mountain, you don't and can't just pick it all up at once. In order to move that mountain, you must move it one pebble or one rock at a time. In doing that, before you know it, that once impenetrable mountain is no longer in front of you blocking your progression. It is now behind you where it should be. It's out of your way and you are free to move about in ways that are more conducive to having you reach your destination. If you find an option that works better for you, then by all means use it. The main objective here is to find a way to have no excuses only results when it comes to following your plan.

A.   CHUCKING WITH MINI STEPS –TABLE OF CONTENTS

One way to attack your reconstruction process is to think back to the days when you had to put together a book report with a table of contents. Each chapter had a heading and then under each heading you had subheadings that signaled what would be addressed in that section of your report. This same approach can be used to break down your ultimate goals into easily manageable parts. Within these parts it will also become easier to track successes within the work or steps completed. Also, it will allow you to see what section(s) either need more time and work or need to be broken down into smaller subsections. This approach, as with the others to be discussed, can be used to address future goals you address in all areas of life. Remember these approaches are hopefully going to become an important part of your habits on how to tackle the mountains you may encounter as you continue to make your life great!

In illustrating how to incorporate this approach into your metamorphosis, I will give you an example as to how to set this up. Remember keep journaling! It helps to truly make sense of everything you are doing, attempting, have completed and it shows your growth.

So, let's say for example, your goal was to lose weight to feel better about your health and appearance. We can all agree that tackling something like that, when done with seriousness, takes more than just missing a few meals and taking the stairs. For true weight loss and maintenance of results, your actions must be such that all you do becomes habit and a part of your life. Your vices on food, exercise, limiting stress, triggers and other things must be taken into consideration. We all have attempted diets at some point in our lives and without the proper planning we fall short. In utilizing the "chunking method" we could set up our weight loss plan as follows:

Ultimate Goal- 50 lb. Weight Loss

Step 1- Reasons Weight Loss Is Necessary

   a. My health is suffering

- High blood pressure
- Diabetes runs in my family
- My cholesterol is high
- I have shortness of breath
- Sleep apnea

Step 2 – Figuring Out Comfortable Size

   a. Ideal Size
- Have been "this size" before
- Easily maintainable size
- Being "this size" benefits my health

Step 3 - Known Triggers That Affect My Weight

   a. Stress at work

   b. Stress with spouse

   c. Chemical Changes within my body

- Period (ladies)
- Low testosterone levels (men)
- Medications
- Age

      d. Boredom

Step 4 - Exercise and Diet Plan

    a._____

       ▪ _____

       ▪ _____

With the chunking method, you are also able to use it like a chart that can be checked off once each step has been completed. By the way, "chunking" means putting your goals in chunks. It allows you to modify or add in steps that need to be made smaller or forgotten in the construction of your goal and its components. The key here is that things are laid out simplistically for you in the hopes of not making this life change a frightful experience. It shouldn't be looked at as insurmountable for that too keeps you frozen in place leading to my mantra: Procrastination + Lack of Motivation = STAGNATION! Stagnation is the antithesis of forward movement, progression, and your ultimate success. It is time to stop looking in the rearview mirror and wondering why you keep crashing. The only time you look in the rearview mirror is to see how far you've come. So, no looking back in nervousness! Take a deep breath and say to yourself, "onward and upward!" You are a success story just waiting to be written.

B.   Alternating Steps- Easy/Hard or Hard/Easy

This step is as easy as it sounds. If you're not up for the Chunking/Table of Contents approach you can simply, after fully committing to the goal at hand, write down the steps that you have committed to take to make your dream goal your tangible reality. However, there are different advantages to either following your steps in the Easy/Hard or Hard/Easy framework. Formulating and completing your steps using the Easy/Hard framework is simple and should probably be used by those who need a little push in getting started.

When an easy step is completed, it allows you to see that in fact, tasks are capable of being accomplished. It gives you a sense of being able to see the effort you are making. This, in turn, provides you with the immediate motivation to not only want to reach your goal but to also give you the push needed to accomplish the hard task that is yet to come. It's a way of celebrating the small victories in your battle that lead to winning the war, so to speak. So, beginning with smaller and easier tasks will give you a quick return on your investment and builds up the excitement to add more victories to your portfolio. It's also not as labor-intensive in the writing department as the first example, but it still needs to be written just like every other relevant and important part of this journey of deconstruction and reconstruction.

Now let's look at the "vice versa" or the Hard/Easy step construction and completion. In approaching your steps in this manner, it also gives you the sense of accomplishment needed to want to move to and through other steps. However, it also, after the grueling part of completing the harder steps first, offers you a small respite when looking at the upcoming easy steps to follow as a vacation or cakewalk compared to the hard step you just completed.

It supplies you with a well-deserved pat on the back as you marvel in amazement at the fact that you did not give up. It shines a light on the fact that you kept persevering through the step and proved to yourself that you are stronger than you once thought or realized. It's as if you left the football huddle, ran out on the field before all those menacing players on the opposing team and still we were unshaken.

You ran the ball in after dodging your opponents and scored. Now doing this approach does or may stretch out the time in which you are able to celebrate a small victory, but delayed gratification is not a bad thing. It helps build your patience, solidifies your investment in what you are trying to do, and the afterglow of the victory is glorious! To conquer the first step means that your commitment to this reconstruction must be deep not just in talk but in vision, feeling, motivation and action. Perseverance must be a key ingredient for you to have for you to get up if you are knocked down. Don't let your "right now" be yours forever! Isn't this the reason you decided to tear down and rebuild?

C.   Buddying Up

We all need encouragement especially when we are charting unfamiliar waters. We have life vests and dinghies for a reason. They help us to survive, to stay afloat. When we are in fear of drowning or need help, they are there.

This is new to you. You may need your personal cheerleader or your motivational megaphone which is that person who will breathe life into you when you are lifeless. You will need that person who will put a mirror to your face and show you your successes as well as bring to your attention where you may be lacking. Hey, Popeye had his spinach, right? His chief nemesis Brutus may have been bigger and always tried to get the better of little Popeye, but when he ate that spinach, Brutus did not have a chance in Hades against him.

So, find yourself some spinach and keep it around. Note: please make sure your "spinach" is of an organic nature for I would hate for you to consume spinach thinking it's going to help you when in all actuality ingesting that off-brand "spinach" may be poisoning you. In plain translation, make sure your accountability buddy is genuine. Make sure that he or she has your best interest at heart and your success means just as much to them as it does to you. Choose someone whose words and actions come from a place of love without tearing you down, but of building you up when they must check you when you are slacking off.

Many times, we choose people to come into our lives whose words are like breath to our lungs and food to our souls. Pay attention because what they may be doing without even realizing it is using that place in our lives to poison us. Sometimes it's done because they too have been fed poison and it's the only way they know how to feed others. Some may just be like the crabs in a bucket or users of your kindness. Those people are the ones that must be put on restriction during and after your rebuilding.

Don't be hurt or surprised when you elevate, and people fall away. Some people in your life are only meant to stay around for a season; not a lifetime. Some people in your life are meant to stay around long enough to poured into and provided you with what they were supposed to whether it was good or bad.

You will not have to end your relationship with them; it will just fade away. It is just their time to move along. Some will simply change to go on their own journey and some end themselves for personal reasons, but whatever the reason, let them go. You can't keep opening windows when God closes doors. Even a slight breeze through a window can bring in the stench from outside that does not need to be inside your house or inside of you. No lamenting just building. If you remember that everything is in divine order, you will see how every step in your life just falls in place.

So, to wrap up this chapter, I want to do a simple recap of what is needed to progress in your reconstruction:

1. Construct your steps in a way that will continue to create intrinsic value and motivation towards achieving your goals.
2. Make sure your steps are achievable. Do not set goals that may be unattainable due to time or resources. It will set you up for failure.
3. It is better to re-assess and re-adjust goals as needed to ensure success. Readjusting and/or reassessing is not a fancy way of saying you failed. It is quite the opposite. It shows you are a dedication to yourself and your reconstruction. It speaks to your perseverance and persistence. You are keeping your eyes on the prize and that's good.
4. Celebrate your successes! Every inch is an inch you didn't have before. Every accomplishment, no matter the size is an accomplishment you didn't have before. It is a step in the positive direction of your reconstruction. Throw out the mindset that celebrating yourself is wrong. It's funny, we celebrate everyone else, but many times when it is

our time for accolades, we have but a small crowd of one. Well, maybe it's time to turn that appreciation inwards. Who knows, others may join your self-celebration once they see that you are worthy of the adoration, attention, and effort.

5. Keep journaling and never stop! Keep a journal of your successes and your thoughts. This allows you to be able to go back and relive the happy moments especially when motivation is lacking, and your mind isn't as focused as it should be. This provides easily accessible motivation and inspiration that will continue to lead you towards your transformation.

6. Buddy up! Get yourself a "Motivational Cheerleader", an accountability partner. Someone who not only celebrates with you but who also provides the "check-in service" meaning they check in on you as well as "check you" on any areas that you may feel unmotivated and may be slacking off. They are truly and unselfishly invested in your success. Hey, if you don't have anyone, I'm available.
   You can personally reach out to me and I'll gladly help! (No, I really mean it. My information is on the back cover of the book,).

7. Only look backward to view your progress and not to regress!! We don't do negative reflection; we do positive progress inspection or step re-visitation, but never, never ever to dwell on the things that will keep us dwelling in the land of stagnation and procrastination!

*Just a suggestion... get some sticky notes and post affirmations, successes, ideas, positive compliments, visions and self-discoveries all over surfaces that you use daily. Mirrors, refrigerators, desks, computer monitors, EVERYWHERE! Let's keep the positive energy, thoughts, and motivation up front and center. Let's ingrain it in your life.

I AM SO EXCITED FOR YOU! LOOK AT YOU!! YOU'RE ON YOUR WAY!

Chapter 7

Your Devine Reflection: Affirmations And Positive Thoughts

"I Am Now Putting My Life In Order Preparing To Accept All The Good That Is Coming To Me"

~ OMG Quotes

Now you have a blueprint about how you are going to tackle the steps associated with reaching your goal of reconstruction. You now have an idea about what you want your manifesto to be. You also have some idea about how to structure your chapters and verses. Now truth time; although you are excited, guess what? I know you probably feel some level of fear. Fear of the unknown, fear of failure. That's all natural and honestly, if you didn't feel some level of retention or fear, I'd worry about how seriously you are taking this process. So, embrace the fear. Yes, feel it, remember it, then change its definition. Now let's look at the word fear and let's give it a new meaning. Fear now stands for Face Everything And Reconstruct!

You are going to use the power of that fear. The same fear that causes you to stop in your tracks and paralyzes you in many ways to the point that you do nothing. You will now harness that same power to propel yourself forward. Instead of fearing what may happen on this journey which will cause you to stall, you will now use that fear and say to yourself, "What will happen to the rest of my life if I don't rebuild/reconstruct?" That should be scarier than moving on to something different. Let's face it, if you do more of the same, you will get more of the same and that is a major reason for this undertaking. You don't want more of the same.

Some of you may have even looked at a calendar, thought about events for things that are approaching and decided to "pick a day" that would be "perfect" to start. It's understandable, but ask yourself this... are you using this "start date" because it's really a perfect time to start or are you simply giving yourself more time to live in your comfort zone? To live in your fear of having to step out and step up? Be honest when answering this because some can't. How can you be completely honest with others if you can't at least be honest with yourself?

Now there may be legitimate reasons about why one day is better to begin to put your plan in motion to start your tangible reconstruction and begin your manifesto, but what makes that day any better than any other to begin? In all actuality, there is never a perfect time to begin most things we set out to undertake. So, let's not put off tomorrow what we can do today. Start small, however, the key is to start.

Who is going to drive this vehicle of change? The answer is the only person with the keys to start the engine and that person is you. These last few chapters are going to be dedicated to your spirit. They are going to be dedicated to helping you not only push through to your strength, progress, worth, beauty and your importance. When you have no one there in those quiet times, when you need encouragement and reminders about why you chose to do this, look back over the pages of this and other chapters of this book. Carry it with you (especially this part) when you know you will encounter situations, people, triggers, stress lures or anything that may knock you off your game.

Now I'm not saying that every day is going to be easy, but conversely, I'm not saying that every day will be hard. However, what I am saying is always to be armed with the tools you need to succeed.

As you go through your daily life, things can come out of left field. Remember it's you who is changing not your elements and your environment. Well, at least not in one fell swoop. The same stressors, people, employment, engagements and everything in between are still going to be very much a part of your daily reality. As you change, these things will go against your normal comfort zone. Many times, we must become uncomfortable to ultimately find where we are meant to be comfortable.

If this book is too cumbersome to carry with you, then attach those sticky notes all over your environment. Stick them on your mirrors, refrigerators, picture frames, bedposts, nightstands, desks at work, inside drawers, sun visors in your car, everywhere you are destined to automatically look during the day. What you are doing is changing your mind to change your behavior which will lead to a change in your perceptions about who you are and what you bring to your daily section of the world. Let's get to it.

Here you will find your Motivational Affirmations Glossary or your M.A.G. for short. Below I will list motivational affirmations that you can look at and commit to memory. You can use some or all of them. The choice is yours. Place them on an empty calendar and each day, live one, share one, but by all means do NOT forget them. They are like the gasoline to your motivational car, the motivational peanut butter to your daily jelly. In simpler terms, they go along with your reconstruction journey. Make them a part of your blueprint that you put together. Incorporate them into your steps, share them if you want and add your own affirmations. Do whatever you have to do to keep you focused. As you conquer steps towards your reconstruction, you will feel inspired and profound thoughts and observations will come to your mind. I suggest you write them down.

I hope that you find some if not all these positive thoughts and affirmations to become of great help to you. I made sure to take my time to build these because again your progress is important.

DAILY POSITIVE THOUGHTS AND AFFIRMATIONS

1. The only thing that can stop me is me.
2. Procrastination + Lack of Motivation =Stagnation.
3. Don't let your "right now" be your forever! You will persevere!
4. Being me is beyond good enough.
5. Changing my thoughts will change my perception and changing my perception will change my behaviors.
6. Don't ask for permission, being your OWN authority.
7. Problems are the pebbles that lead me to perfection.
8. I am stronger than the situations that try to compound to me.
9. "Can't" just means that you won't – prove yourself wrong today!
10. I am the builder of my beliefs and the director of my dreams.
11. Nothing will happen if I will it so.
12. Today is the day I put myself first and my fears last.
13. Work is inevitable, but so is a failure if I fail to work.
14. I am stronger than my struggles, bigger than my burdens and worth more than my worries.

15. I am a minor of diamonds for I once was but a lump of coal.
16. Today is mine to behold and mind to control.
17. I will live life instead of letting life live me.
18. I am better than I was and greater than I once believed.
19. If success is to be mine, then my mind and actions must seek success.
20. I am deserving of my desires and set up for success.
21. My love for myself is greater than the hate that surrounds me.
22. I will not give in for giving in is giving up on me.
23. I will celebrate my successes no matter how small
24. If I give in I will give up and that is not an option.
25. I MATTER, NO MATTER WHAT!
26. I am not who they say I am, but who I believe I am to be.
27. I am a great gift and able to accomplish great things.
28. There is nobody better at being me than ME.
29. Every step I take leads me to my destination. I will order my steps wisely.
30. I am worthy of all the joys I see others enjoy.
31. I hold the key to unlock the prison I voluntarily keep myself in.

32. I choose my direction and hold the power of progress.
33. To get what I never had I need to do things I've never done.
34. BREATHE! FOCUS! PROCEED! REPEAT!
35. My reflection is my only competition.
36. I will not let fear keep me from my freedom.
37. My process will take patience, but I am worth the wait!
38. If you will it, so it will be. I will myself happiness, for happiness lies within me.
39. Consistency breeds results whereas inconsistency breeds repeats.
40. Every day I am closer to the me I always wanted to be.
41. I am not who I used to be and soon I will be even better than I am.
42. I am growing for I am now feeding myself acceptance, love, positivity, and fearlessness.
43. I am stronger than I realize and better than I admit.
44. I am only as good as my last success. Keep going!
45. Keep going. Keep GROWING!
46. The only power others have over me is the power I willingly give to them.
47. No longer will I be sick and tired. Now I will be positive and inspired!

48. I am strong enough to face it all for only winners rise from a fall.
49. Change happens when chances are taken.
50. I will acknowledge my negative emotions and let them go. If I stay captured by them, my progress will be slow.
51. I am allowed to be happy.
52. If I rush the process the results will disappear just as fast.
53. I am Unique, Unstoppable and Under Construction.
54. I am more than enough and less than too much.
55. Direction comes when distractions fade.

Chapter 8

You Are The Phoenix Rising From The Ashes

"And just like the Phoenix rose from the ashes, she too will rise. Returning from the flames, clothed in nothing but her strength, more beautiful than ever before."

~Shannen Heartzs

This last chapter is going to be dedicated to reinforcing where you've been and who you are becoming. It is meant to pour into your spirit more vivid images from which to identify your transformation. Hopefully, by this point, you are well on your way to your reconstruction. However, if by chance you are still on the fence, it is my hope that seeing yourself as the mythical Phoenix will help to put more fire in your soul and place more perspective on what it is that needs to be done.

I'm sure you've heard the saying, "...like a phoenix rising from the ashes." It usually comes up when life starts to feel like your very foundation is being rocked. You will feel like something just knocked you to the ground turning your heart, soul, situation, hopes, and dreams to ashes. Those ashes smolder on top of us and bury us. Sometimes the ashes and rubble are light, meaning the casualties or the fall out isn't too hard to rectify. However, then we have those explosions that leave shrapnel so heavy that we wonder how, if ever, will we get from under it. You ask yourself how will I rise above it all and again reclaim my life, my hopes, and dreams? How can I stop the hurt of having to see the forest for the trees in dealing with the truth of what lies ahead? For it is far easier to move on without sifting through the destruction to take the lessons and truths with you.

The truth is if we don't do that, we run the risk of repeating the same mistakes by rebuilding our lives with the ashes and rubble that still lie before us. What we also neglect to see is that if we continue to do the rebuilding with the shoddy materials that buried us, even though the materials are familiar and feel like home, we limit ourselves from continuing to elevate from our tiny shack to our brand-new mansions. You can't build a new and upgraded mansion if you continue to use the same outdated and overused materials you continue to use to build your apartment. The materials are not of the same quantity or quality.

The choice to move, to rise above, to let go, flap your wings and soar like the mystical being you are is all your own. Sometimes you must realize that being uncomfortable is temporary because it's transporting you to where you are meant to be forever comfortable.

As the story or myth is told, the Phoenix is a mythical bird with fiery feathers and a lifespan of 100 years. As it nears the end of its life, it settles into its nest which catches fire and burns fiercely. As it burns, it reduces the nest and the Phoenix to ashes. From those ashes a new Phoenix arises – renewed and reborn. If we break down this mythical tale, there lies an example about how we rise above the destruction when problems arise.

Let's begin with the obvious, the mythical Phoenix. This bird, the Phoenix, is you, it is me, it is all of us. We see ourselves the way we perceive ourselves to be. For example, my mythical bird is sleek, with long flowing cobalt blue and black plumage, piercing eyes, long talons, soaring high above the trees. My Phoenix has two voices. The one voice is very melodic and the other is a very loud squawk.

The loud squawk comes out when I experience hurt, pain, betrayal, loss, injustice and even when those I love are hurt or mistreated. Conversely, the beautiful melodic voice sounds when I am happy, feeling joy, love, compassion, comfortable in my skin, accomplished, protected and settled.

Next, let's look at the nest. The nest is our home base. Our sanctuary from which we derive our comfort. The nest catching fire and burning to ashes as well as the Phoenix translates into problems, hardships, abandonment, and fractured relationships coming into our nest, our lives, our hearts and souls. When this happens, it ultimately decimates our nest. It burns us, it burns what we've made, what we cherish, what we believe to be real and as it burns it takes with it all that made us our old Phoenix. The burning lays us bare. This is when the choice must be made to either stay in the ashes or rise from the ashes and soar. When you rise from the ashes, rise bigger, better, stronger, wiser, and more importantly smarter. Going through that metamorphosis is supposed to bring about change. If we embrace the fire and destruction this is what gives us the chance of emerging as a new and improved version of ourselves.

When we emerge, we emerge knowing what to let go of and what no longer is serving our greater good. We grow smarter in the ways of knowing the truth when we see it, in trusting ourselves enough to know to listen and do what is right for us. Smarter in knowing how to not only rebuild our nests but in how to rebuild ourselves.

From the burning of your plumage, and being stripped bare, you will come out anew. You will be formed into the diamond you are from the lump of coal you once were.

There is no time to procrastinate and wallow in the ashes. You are to use those ashes to motivate yourself to move on, to make things better using your own words, self-respect, authentic truths and lessons you've just been given. Don't remain stagnant. Don't rebuild using the same situations, thoughts or people who led you down your current path. No one is going to build or rebuild your nest or your life as perfectly as you will for yourself. When those people come along with their ideas and their "building permits", take a second to look at where they are living first and the materials they used to build their own dwellings and see if that is what you want your nest or your life to mimic.

We look at problems and situations just as we view a fire from the outside; as total destruction. Although it is true that fire does burns; it also clears away. Ashes smolder, but they cool down and blow away. Life hurts, but it gets better. People hurt, use, lie and abuse, but it is up to you to either stay and take the abuse or go and rebuild what they have torn down. Remember, if you do nothing, then you gain nothing. When all seems lost you can rise like the Phoenix. What defines all of us is how well we rise after falling. Trust this healing and rebuilding process. Sometimes you must die a little inside to be reborn and rise again as a stronger and wiser version of yourself. So, do just that. Rise! If you find yourself in that burning nest, shake the ashes off and soar higher than the destruction left behind. It may hurt, it may cause sleepless nights, horrible replayed visions in your mind, but the longer you stay buried, the longer you hurt. The purpose of this book is to take you out of the hurt.

The time that we spend staying stagnant and living in our pain and suffering, we waste precious moments that we cannot get back. Sometimes it helps to look at it this way... What if you had 24 hours to live? What would you want to try, feel, experience, let go of or take part in during those last hours? What would that urgency activate inside of you?

Hmmmm, 24 hours. I mean really ponder that question. As a matter of fact, let me change that to make it easier for you. What if you went to your doctor or better yet GOD himself and he said to you, "My child you have 48 hours left on Earth." Let that sink in. And here are a few questions for you to ponder: What would be your first feelings? Would you try to barter or beg for more time? Then, after it all sinks in, what would your first move be? Would you drain your bank account enjoying things that you've always wanted or deserved but put off? Would you take a redeye to an exotic locale that was on your bucket list? Would you go to work and give people a piece of your mind? Let them know *exactly* how you feel? Would you commit a crime because basically, what the heck, if you get caught, you won't be in jail for too long? You just wanted to feel the excitement and thrill of it all because you only have 48 hours. Maybe you would gather those closest to you, those who you fought with, and those who once meant the world to you, to make amends because now you're realizing that each day of life is not promised. The thought of leaving the earth without saying those words, righting those wrongs, saying what's on your heart to someone you love to let them know that even though you will not be there physically, your love for them was made clear.

Now I know that this may have put a damper on your feelings and your outlook, but I have a point. The point is it would be easier to know if you had 24 or 48 hours left because then you could begin to do all the things that you continue to put off. All those things that you felt you had time to do. Maybe those things didn't seem important or maybe you were just too afraid to accomplish them whatever they may be. In getting the news that you must wrap it all up propels you to right the wrongs and live to the fullest.

Here is another scenario... What if you had 24 or 48 hours to live and you didn't know? You continued to put off tomorrow what you should have done today? Those things that, especially when they relate to you personally, didn't seem as important or as imperative or as much fun at the moment because you felt you had time. Now I'm not saying this to make anyone depressed, upset or nervous. Although I think getting checkups is very important, I am not saying this to make you run out to the doctor or the hospital now to check on your health. I am saying all this to say that life is short and dreams, hopes, relationships, and aspirations should not always be put off because tomorrow is not promised. When you have the seeds inside of you and you feel as if you can plant them at any time and they can take root, it causes us to forget that they are even there. Then when the time comes, and you leave this earth, all your gifts, dreams, aspirations, hopes, and things that needed to be said, leave this earth with you.

Time is something that is free and at the same time priceless. It's free in that it is given to us each day that we are blessed with being able to wake up. Even if we miss our coffee, time was still given to you. Time is a present, so it is important to live in the present.

However, it is also priceless because no amount of money will allow anyone to buy back the time that they have wasted.

This book and my hope are to put a light up to your face and into your spirit to allow you to see that just like time is priceless, you are as well. Just as the free time that you were given in the past that you may have spent living in a place of despair, uncertainty, just getting by, wanting but not attempting, talking yourself out of and spending its expensive essence on others and their situations. The present time and your future should not be spent foolishly on everything and everyone else while neglecting all that you are and all that you are set to become.

Everything may not be great, but in everything, something great can be found. So, now is the time to find and reconstruct YOU! If you must reread this entire book again or certain parts, so be it. Keep the process and the progression at the forefront of your mind. Keep the fires burning in your spirit. Do whatever is needed to keep this train of progression moving for the moment you lose sight of it you risk derailment.

You are worth it. You are amazing. The deconstruction may have been and may continue to be difficult, but the reconstruction will be beautiful.

Dr. Samone is out.......

Made in the USA
Middletown, DE
29 August 2018